Folk Dance

Marjorie Seevers

xist Publishing

Check out all of the books in the Dancing Through Life Series

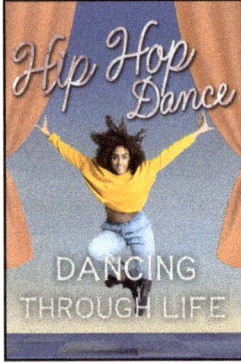

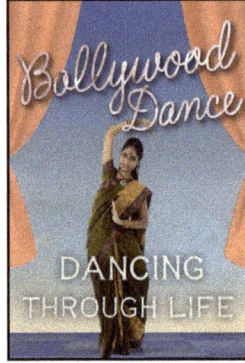

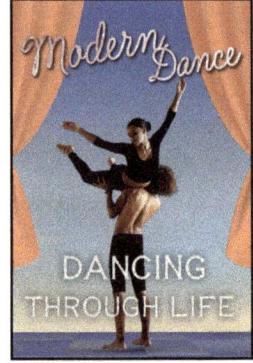

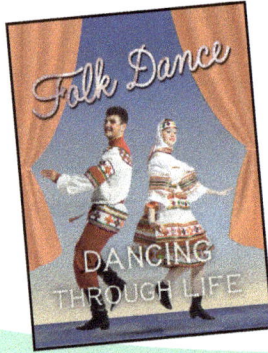

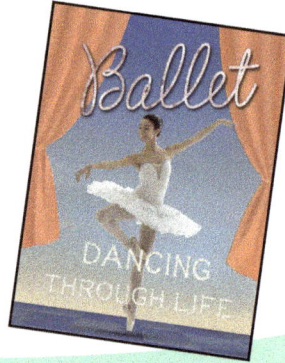

Published in the United States by Xist Publishing
www.xistpublishing.com
© 2025 Copyright Xist Publishing

All images licensed from Adobe Stock

First Edition
Hardcover ISBN: 978-1-5324-5445-5
Paperback ISBN: 978-1-5324-5446-2
eISBN: 978-1-5324-5444-8

PUBLISHED IN TEXAS

Contents

DANCING
THROUGH
LIFE

Chapter 1: What is Folk Dance?

Folk dance is a type of dance that comes from local culture. These dances are passed down from parents to children. Folk dances are often part of everyday life, celebrations, and stories.

Each country, and sometimes each region, has its own folk dances. For example, in Ireland, people perform céilí dance. This is a group dance enjoyed at social events. In Mexico, dancers perform the Jarabe Tapatío, also called the Mexican Hat Dance. In the United States, square dancing is a folk dance that brings people together.

Folk dances are usually done in groups. The dancers form circles, lines, or pairs. The movements are simple and easy to learn, so everyone can join in. Folk dances are often performed at festivals, weddings, and other events.

One special thing about folk dance is that it tells a story. The steps and movements show important parts of life. They might represent planting crops, celebrating a good harvest, or marking a special event. Through folk dance, people share their culture and traditions.

Folk dance is a fun way to connect with others and celebrate culture. It's a dance for everyone, no matter your age or skill level. When you learn a folk dance, you join a tradition enjoyed for many years.

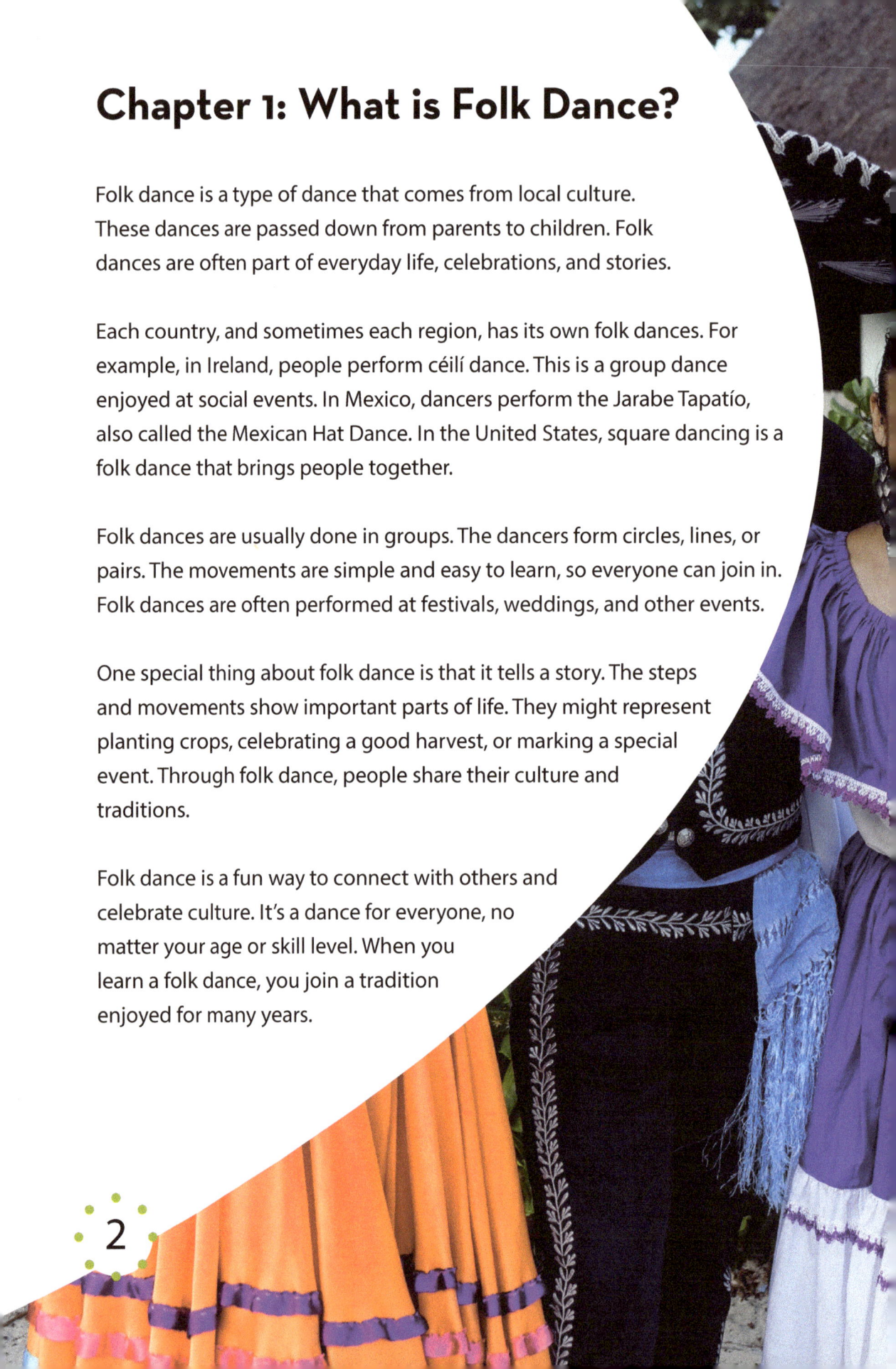

The History of Folk Dance: A Dance for the People

Folk dance has been around for a very long time. It began when people wanted to celebrate, tell stories, or mark special events. Unlike dances in royal courts or big theaters, folk dance is for everyone. It was created by regular people and shared with their communities.

Long ago, people lived in small villages. They worked hard every day, but they also found time to dance. These dances were simple and easy to learn. They often showed parts of daily life, like farming, fishing, or celebrating a good harvest. Dancing together made people feel close and happy.

Different regions created their own folk dances. Each dance showed what was important to that group of people. For example, in some places, dances were about nature, like rivers or mountains. In other places, they were about work, like planting crops or weaving.

As time passed, these dances were passed down from one generation to the next. Parents taught their children, and those children taught their own kids. This way, the dances stayed alive and became a strong part of each culture.

Folk dance has always been a way for people to come together. It doesn't matter if you are young or old, rich or poor. Everyone can join in a folk dance. That's why it's called a dance for the people. Folk dances have been enjoyed for hundreds of years, and they are still danced today, keeping the tradition alive.

Who Can Be a Folk Dancer?

Anyone can be a folk dancer! Folk dance is for everyone, no matter your age, background, or skill level. It doesn't matter where you come from or how much experience you have. If you enjoy moving to music and being part of a group, you can be a folk dancer.

Folk dances are often simple and easy to learn. This makes them perfect for beginners. You don't need to be a trained dancer or know special steps to join in. Many people learn folk dances by watching others and practicing together.

Folk dance is also a great way to bring people together. In many communities, folk dances are performed at festivals, weddings, and other special events. These dances are a fun way to celebrate and connect with others. Everyone can join in, from young children to grandparents.

In some places, folk dances are taught in schools. Students learn about their culture through dance. They might even perform folk dances at school events. This helps keep the tradition alive and allows young people to be a part of it.

Folk dance is about more than just dancing. It's about being part of a community and sharing a tradition. Whether you are dancing in a small village or a big city, folk dance brings people together. So, who can be a folk dancer? The answer is simple: anyone who wants to join in the fun!

The Different Roles in Folk Dance

In folk dance, everyone has an important role. Whether you are dancing alone, with a partner, or in a group, each role adds something special to the dance.

One role in folk dance is the lead dancer. The lead dancer often starts the dance and helps guide the other dancers. They might show the steps or call out directions. The lead dancer needs to be confident and know the dance well.

Partner dancing is common in many folk dances. In this role, two dancers work together. They might hold hands, link arms, or dance side by side. Partner dancing is about teamwork and moving in sync with each other.

Group dancing is another important part of folk dance. In a group dance, many dancers move together. They might form circles, lines, or other shapes. Group dancing shows unity and the strength of the community. Each dancer in the group helps to create a beautiful and lively performance.

In some folk dances, there is a role for callers or leaders. These people don't dance but instead guide the dancers. They might call out the steps or tell the dancers when to change partners. The caller keeps the dance organized and fun.

Solo dancers also have a role in folk dance. Sometimes, a dancer will perform alone in the center of the group. They might show off special steps or movements. The solo dancer often adds excitement and energy to the dance.

Chapter 3: Folk Dance Basics

Basic Steps and Movements

Folk dance steps are often simple and easy to learn. These basic movements help everyone join in and enjoy the dance. Each folk dance has its own steps, but many share some common movements.

One common step is the step-hop. In this move, the dancer steps forward with one foot and then hops on that foot. This step is light and bouncy, adding energy to the dance. The step-hop is often repeated in a pattern, making it easy to follow. Another basic move is the circle dance. In this move, dancers join hands and form a circle. They might move to the left, to the right, or change direction. The circle dance is a symbol of unity and togetherness. It's a common move in many folk dances around the world.

Clapping is another key movement in folk dance. Dancers might clap their hands in time with the music. Clapping adds rhythm and excitement to the dance. Sometimes, dancers clap to greet each other or to mark the end of a dance.

Partner turns are also common in folk dance. In this move, dancers hold hands or link arms and spin around. The turn is usually smooth and graceful, allowing partners to connect and move together. Partner turns add a playful and interactive element to the dance.

In some folk dances, dancers use a stomp or tap to add emphasis. This move is done by bringing one foot down hard on the floor. The stomp or tap makes a strong sound, adding to the rhythm of the dance. It's a way to show energy and enthusiasm. These basic steps and movements are the building blocks of folk dance. They are easy to learn and fun to do. By mastering these steps, dancers can join in and enjoy folk dances from different cultures.

Expressing Culture Through Folk Dance

Folk dance is more than just steps. It's a way to show and share culture. Each folk dance tells something special about the people who created it.

The music used in folk dances is often traditional. It might include drums, fiddles, or flutes. The music shows the culture's history and traditions. In some places, the music is fast and lively, showing joy and celebration. In other places, the music might be slow and graceful, showing respect or a special event.

The costumes worn in folk dances also show culture. Dancers wear clothes that represent their community. The colors, patterns, and designs of the costumes often have special meanings. For example, some costumes use bright colors to show happiness. Others might include patterns that tell stories or show important events.

The stories told through folk dance are another way to show culture. Many folk dances are about daily life, work, or nature. They might show planting crops, fishing, or celebrating a good harvest. These dances help keep the stories and traditions of a culture alive.

Folk dance can also show beliefs and values. Some dances are performed during festivals or religious events. They might honor a god, celebrate the seasons, or mark a special day. Through these dances, people share what is important to them.

By learning and performing folk dances, people can connect with their culture. They can also share their culture with others. Folk dance is a way to celebrate who you are and where you come from. It's a living tradition that brings people together and keeps cultures alive.

Chapter 4: Dressing for Folk Dance

Traditional Folk Dance Outfits: Colors and Styles

Traditional folk dance outfits are important. They show the culture and history of the people who created the dance. The colors, patterns, and styles of these outfits often have special meanings.

In many cultures, bright colors are used in folk dance outfits. These colors show happiness, joy, and celebration. For example, dancers might wear bright red or yellow for festivals or weddings. The bright colors make the dance look lively.

Patterns on the outfits also have meanings. Some patterns tell stories or show important events. A pattern might show flowers, animals, or symbols from the culture. These patterns make the outfits special.

The style of the outfit is important too. In some cultures, dancers wear long skirts that swing when they move. In others, they wear short skirts or pants that let them move quickly. The style of the outfit often matches the type of dance. For example, a dance with lots of spinning might have skirts that twirl.

Accessories like hats, scarves, or belts are often worn with the outfits. These accessories can add meaning to the outfit. For example, a special hat might show that the dancer has a certain role in the dance. A scarf might be used to make the movements look more graceful.

Traditional folk dance outfits are more than just clothes. They are a way to show pride in a culture. The colors, patterns, and styles make the dance more beautiful. When dancers wear these outfits, they are telling a story and sharing their culture.

Accessories and Props in Folk Dance

In folk dance, accessories and props are important. They add to the look and feel of the dance. These items can also help tell a story or show the culture of the dance.

Hats are a common accessory in many folk dances. Dancers might wear special hats to show their role in the dance. For example, a wide-brimmed hat might be worn in a dance about farming. The hat adds to the story and makes the dance more interesting.

Scarves are often used as props in folk dance. Dancers might wave or twirl scarves as they move. The scarf adds color and movement to the dance. It can also make the dance look more graceful and flowing.

Bells and anklets are sometimes worn by dancers. These items make noise as the dancers move. The jingling sound adds rhythm to the dance. It helps keep the beat and makes the dance more lively.

Ribbons are another popular prop. Dancers might hold ribbons and move them in patterns. The ribbons create shapes in the air, adding a playful element to the dance. Instruments like tambourines or drums can also be used in folk dance. Dancers might play these instruments while they move. This adds music to the dance and helps keep the rhythm.

Props and accessories make folk dance more colorful and fun. They add to the story and help show the culture of the dance. When dancers use these items, they bring the dance to life and make it more enjoyable for everyone.

Chapter 5: The Big Performance

Preparing for the Stage

Getting ready for a folk dance performance is exciting. It takes time and practice to make sure everything goes well. Dancing in front of people is special, and dancers want to give their best performance.

First, dancers practice their moves many times. They learn each step until they can do it without thinking. This practice helps them feel confident and ready. Dancers often rehearse together in a group. This way, they can make sure everyone is in sync.

Next, dancers prepare their costumes and accessories. Each outfit must fit well and be comfortable. Dancers try on their costumes to make sure they can move easily. They also check their accessories, like hats or scarves, to make sure everything is in place.

On the day of the performance, dancers arrive early. They need time to warm up their muscles. Warming up helps prevent injuries and gets their bodies ready to dance. Dancers stretch and do light exercises to prepare.

After warming up, dancers put on their costumes and makeup. Makeup helps make their faces stand out under the stage lights. Dancers might also style their hair to keep it neat during the dance.

Before going on stage, dancers do a final rehearsal. This last practice helps them feel prepared. They go over the hardest parts of the dance. Then, they take a moment to relax and focus. Dancers might take deep breaths to calm their nerves.

Preparing for the stage is a big part of being a dancer. It takes hard work and dedication. But all the effort is worth it when the dancers step into the spotlight and share their dance with the audience, especially at cultural festivals and village celebrations.

The Joy of Performing Folk Dance

Performing folk dance is a joyful experience. After all the practice, it's time to share the dance with others. Folk dancers often perform at cultural festivals and village celebrations, bringing joy to the audience.

When the music starts, dancers feel excitement. They move with energy and rhythm, telling stories through their dance. Each step and movement is done with care. The dancers feel proud of what they have learned.

As they dance, the audience watches closely. The bright costumes and lively music make the performance fun to watch. Dancers connect with the music and the people watching. They show feelings like happiness and celebration through their movements.

Performing in a group adds to the joy. Folk dance is often done with many dancers moving together. This creates a sense of community and teamwork. Each dancer helps make the dance beautiful.

The joy of performing folk dance stays with the dancers even after the show ends. They feel proud and connected to their culture. They know they have shared something special with the audience. This feeling inspires them to keep dancing and share their culture with others.

Hearing applause from the audience makes the dancers feel appreciated. Each clap shows that the audience enjoyed the performance. This makes the dancers feel happy and proud. It shows that all their hard work has paid off.

Conclusion

Folk dance is more than just moving to music. It's a way to share stories, culture, and joy. Through folk dance, people connect with their history and with each other. Each step, movement, and song tells something special about the people who created it.

Folk dance is for everyone. It doesn't matter where you come from or how old you are. Whether you are dancing in a small village or at a big festival, folk dance brings people together. It's a tradition that has been enjoyed for many years and will continue for many more.

When you learn a folk dance, you become part of something bigger. You help keep the stories and traditions alive. You also share the joy of dance with others. Folk dance is a celebration of life, community, and culture.

So, keep dancing, keep learning, and keep sharing. Folk dance is a beautiful way to express yourself and connect with others. It's a dance for everyone, and it's a dance for you.

Glossary

Folk Dance   A traditional dance passed down through generations, reflecting local culture.

Céilí Dance   A group folk dance from Ireland, often performed at social events.

Jarabe Tapatío   A traditional Mexican folk dance also known as the Mexican Hat Dance.

Square Dance   A folk dance from the United States, performed by groups in a square formation.

Step-hop   A common folk dance step involving a step followed by a hop on one foot.

Circle Dance   A folk dance where dancers join hands and move in a circle.

Clapping   A rhythmic hand movement used in folk dance to add excitement and energy.

Partner Turn   A folk dance movement where partners hold hands and spin together.

Costume   Traditional clothing worn in folk dances that reflects cultural heritage.

Caller   A person who guides dancers by calling out the steps in folk dances.

Index